HAUNTED HISTORY

CAN'T REST IN PEACE

by Leah Kaminski

Illustrations by Candy Briones

BEARPORT
PUBLISHING

Minneapolis, Minnesota

Credits

22T: ©Jrappold/Wikimedia; 22B: ©Schlitzer90/Wikimedia

DISCLAIMER: This graphic story is a dramatization based on true events. It is intended to give the reader a sense of the narrative rather than a presentation of actual details as they occurred.

Library of Congress Cataloging-in-Publication Data

Names: Kaminski, Leah, author. | Briones, Candy, 1987– illustrator.
Title: Can't rest in peace / by Leah Kaminski ; illustrated by Candy Briones.
Description: Bear claw. | Minneapolis, Minnesota : Bearport Publishing, [2021] | Series: Haunted history | Includes bibliographical references and index.
Identifiers: LCCN 2020008641 (print) | LCCN 2020008642 (ebook) | ISBN 9781647470104 (library binding) | ISBN 9781647470173 (paperback) | ISBN 9781647470241 (ebook)
Subjects: LCSH: Haunted places–Juvenile literature. | Haunted places–Comic books, strips, etc. | Ghosts–Juvenile literature. | Ghosts–Comic books, strips, etc. | Libraries–Miscellanea–Juvenile literature. | Libraries–Miscellanea–Comic books, strips, etc. | Graphic novels. | Graphic novels.
Classification: LCC BF1471 .K36 2021 (print) | LCC BF1471 (ebook) | DDC 133.1/22–dc23
LC record available at https://lccn.loc.gov/2020008641
LC ebook record available at https://lccn.loc.gov/2020008642

For more information, write to Bearport Publishing, 5357 Penn Avenue South, Minneapolis, MN 55419. Printed in the United States of America.

CONTENTS

HAUNTED LIBRARIES

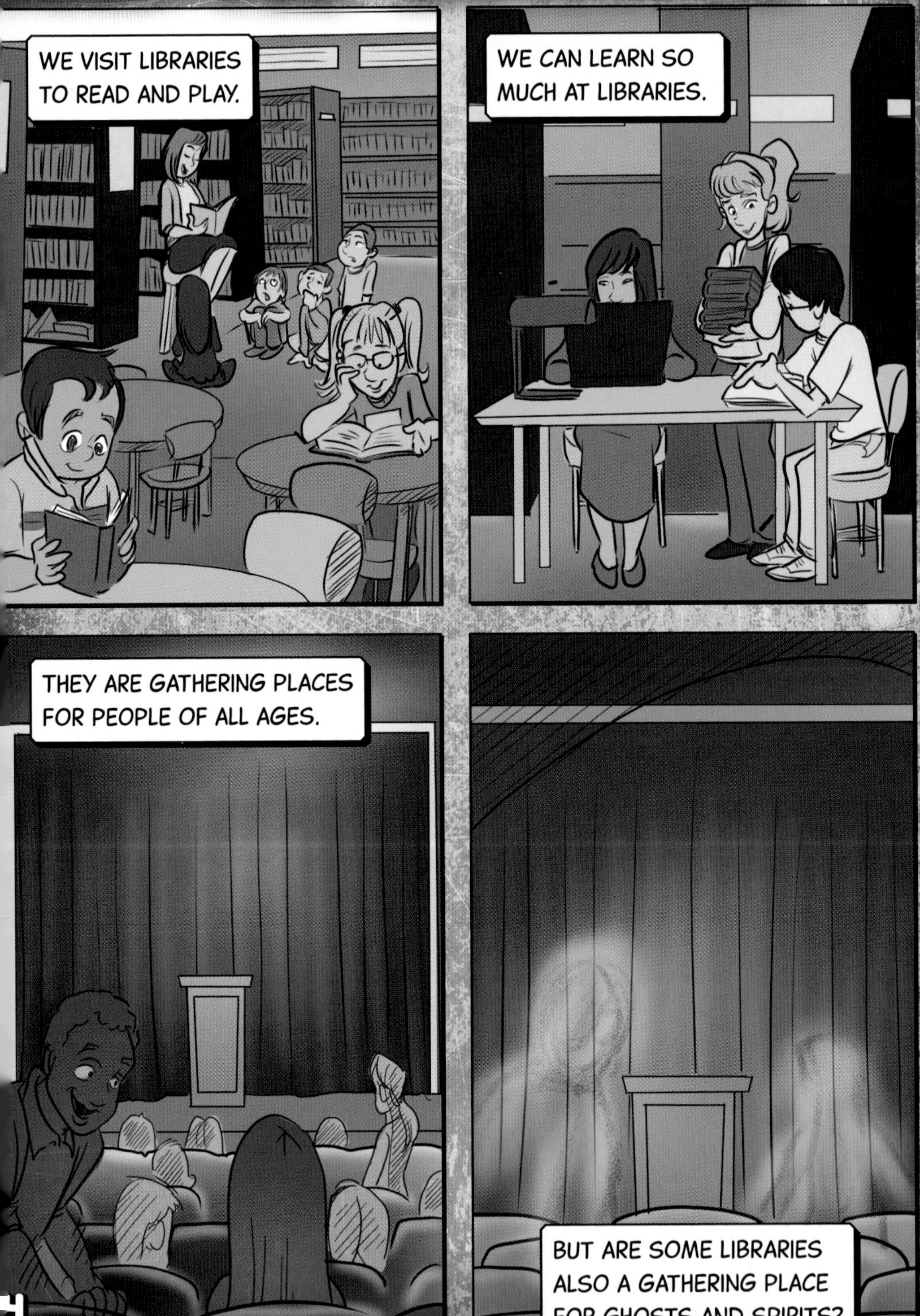
WE VISIT LIBRARIES TO READ AND PLAY.
WE CAN LEARN SO MUCH AT LIBRARIES.
THEY ARE GATHERING PLACES FOR PEOPLE OF ALL AGES.
BUT ARE SOME LIBRARIES ALSO A GATHERING PLACE FOR GHOSTS AND SPIRITS?

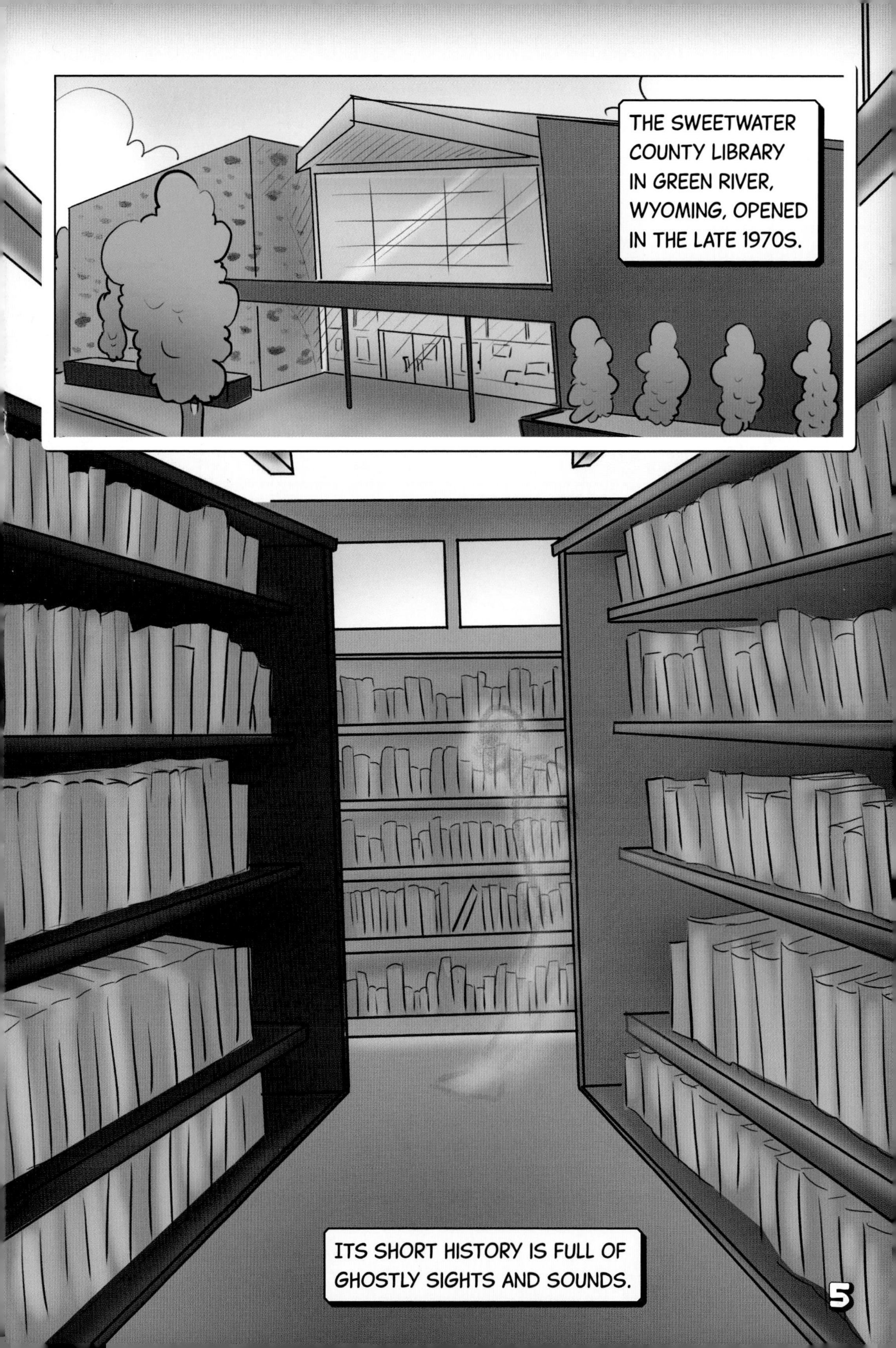
THE SWEETWATER COUNTY LIBRARY IN GREEN RIVER, WYOMING, OPENED IN THE LATE 1970S.
ITS SHORT HISTORY IS FULL OF GHOSTLY SIGHTS AND SOUNDS.

VOICES IN THE DARK

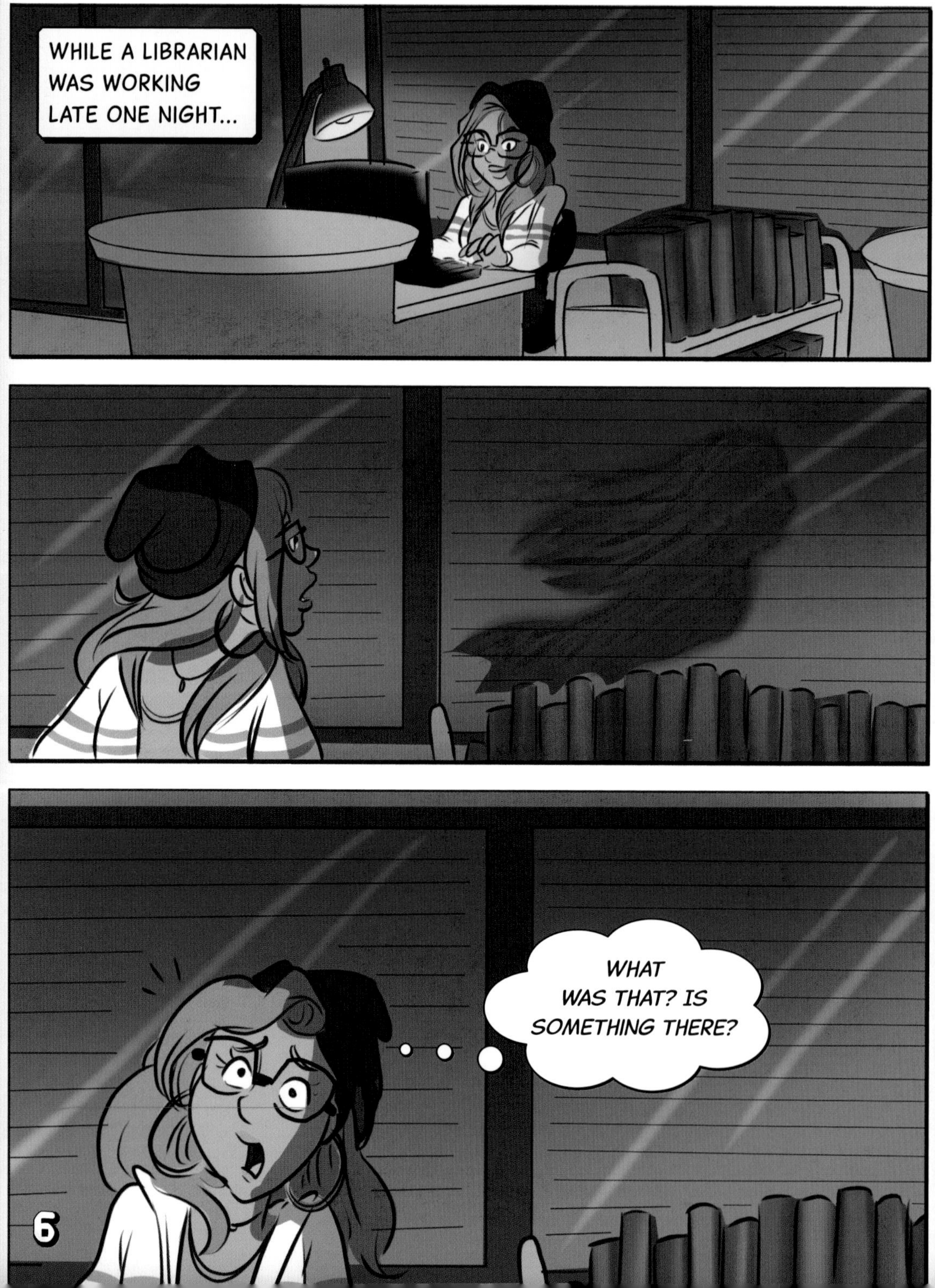
WHILE A LIBRARIAN WAS WORKING LATE ONE NIGHT...
WHAT WAS THAT? IS SOMETHING THERE?

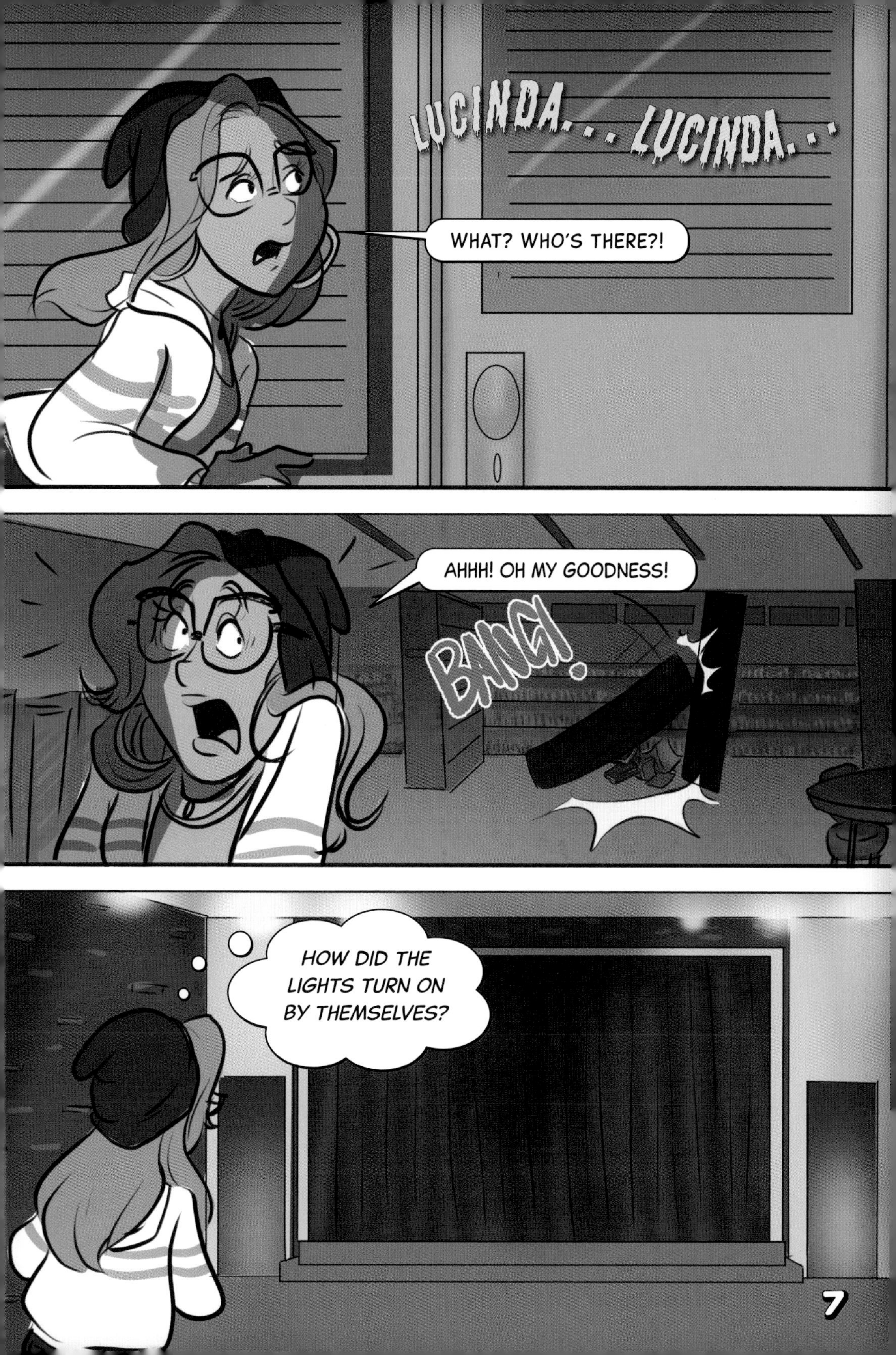
LUCINDA. . . LUCINDA. . .
WHAT? WHO'S THERE?!
AHHH! OH MY GOODNESS!
BANG!
HOW DID THE LIGHTS TURN ON BY THEMSELVES?

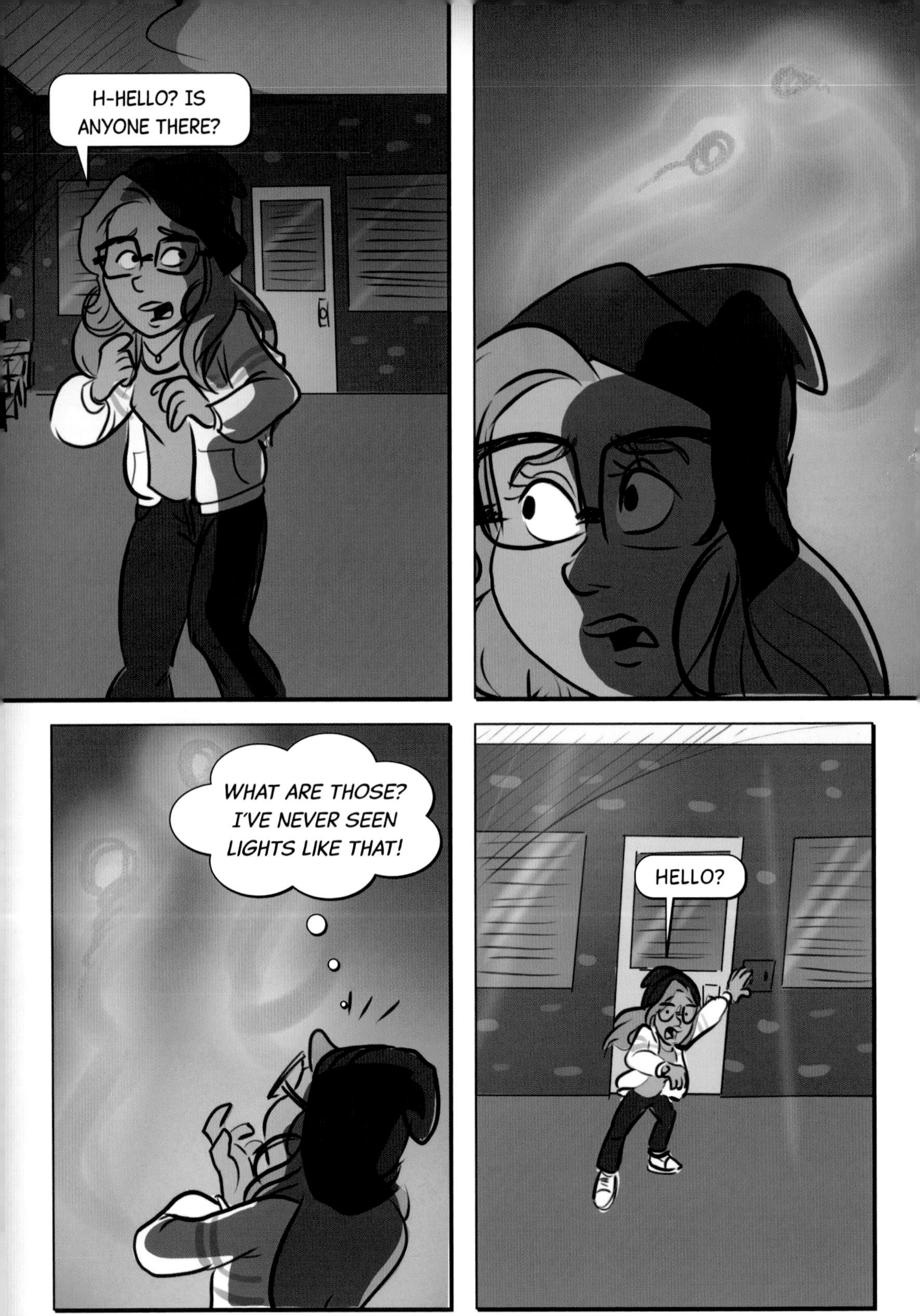
H-HELLO? IS ANYONE THERE?
WHAT ARE THOSE? I'VE NEVER SEEN LIGHTS LIKE THAT!
HELLO?

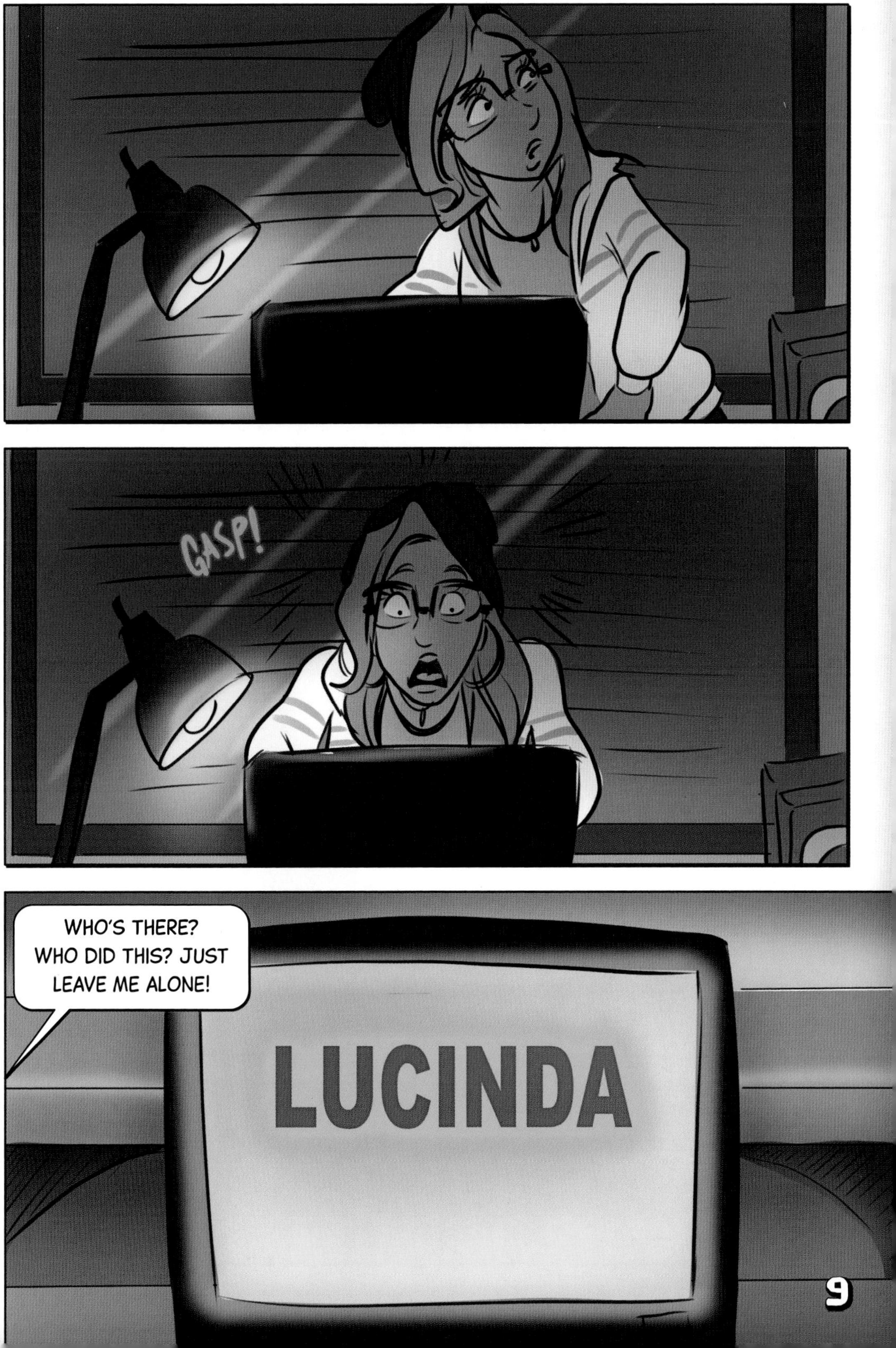
GASP!
WHO'S THERE? WHO DID THIS? JUST LEAVE ME ALONE!
LUCINDA

BONES BELOW

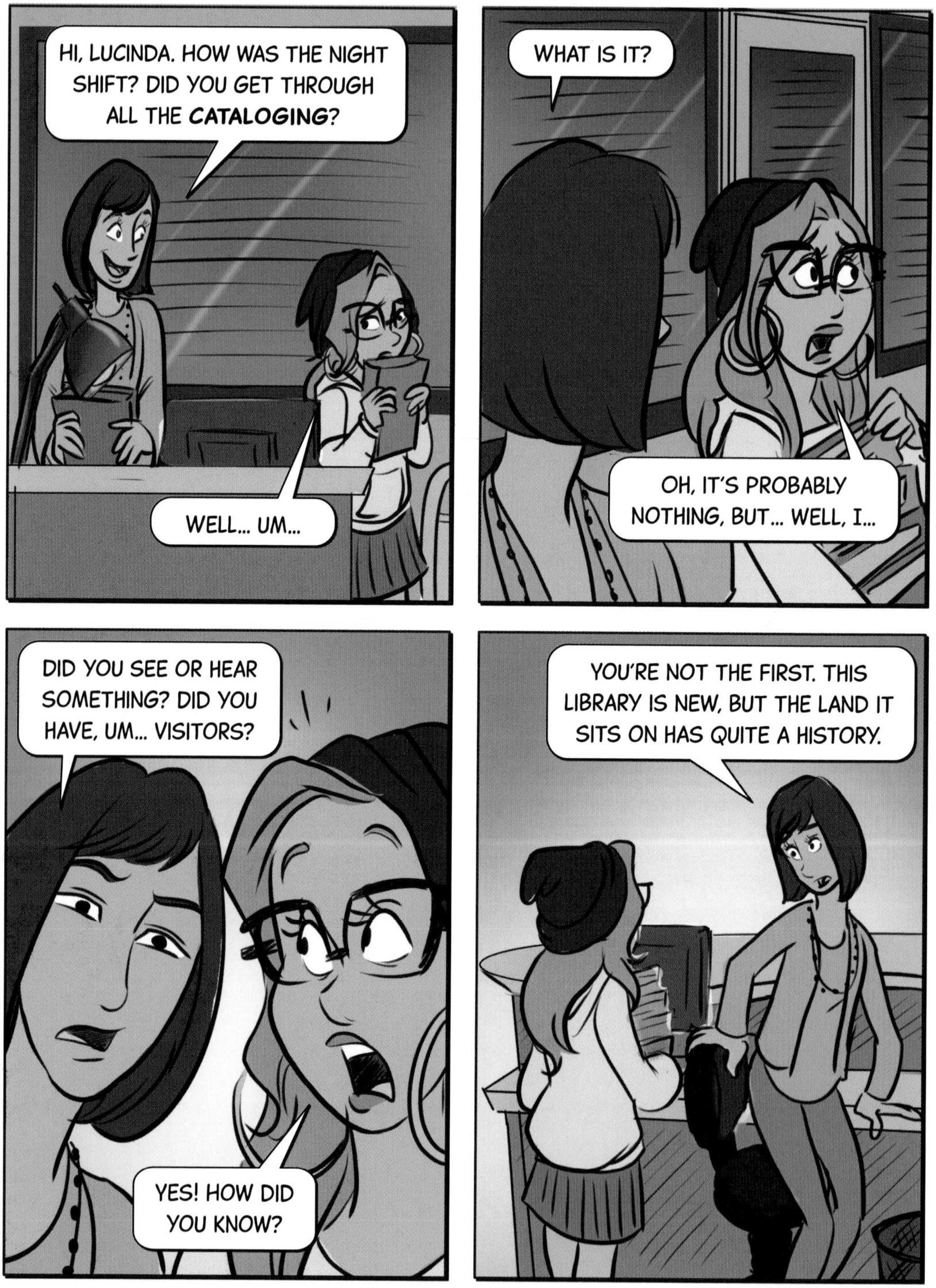
HI, LUCINDA. HOW WAS THE NIGHT SHIFT? DID YOU GET THROUGH ALL THE **CATALOGING**?
WELL... UM...
WHAT IS IT?
OH, IT'S PROBABLY NOTHING, BUT... WELL, I...
DID YOU SEE OR HEAR SOMETHING? DID YOU HAVE, UM... VISITORS?
YES! HOW DID YOU KNOW?
YOU'RE NOT THE FIRST. THIS LIBRARY IS NEW, BUT THE LAND IT SITS ON HAS QUITE A HISTORY.

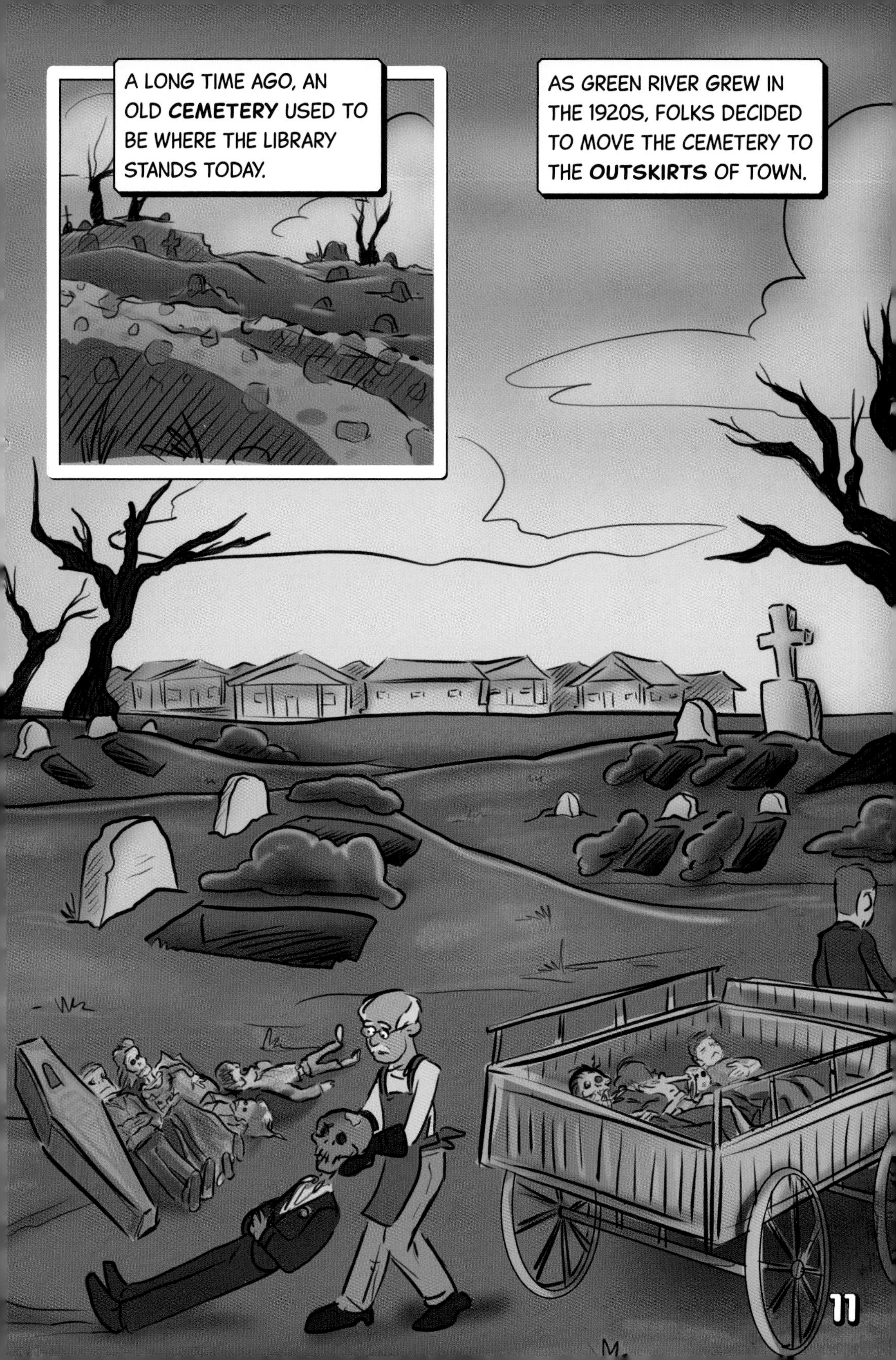
A LONG TIME AGO, AN OLD CEMETERY USED TO BE WHERE THE LIBRARY STANDS TODAY.
AS GREEN RIVER GREW IN THE 1920S, FOLKS DECIDED TO MOVE THE CEMETERY TO THE OUTSKIRTS OF TOWN.

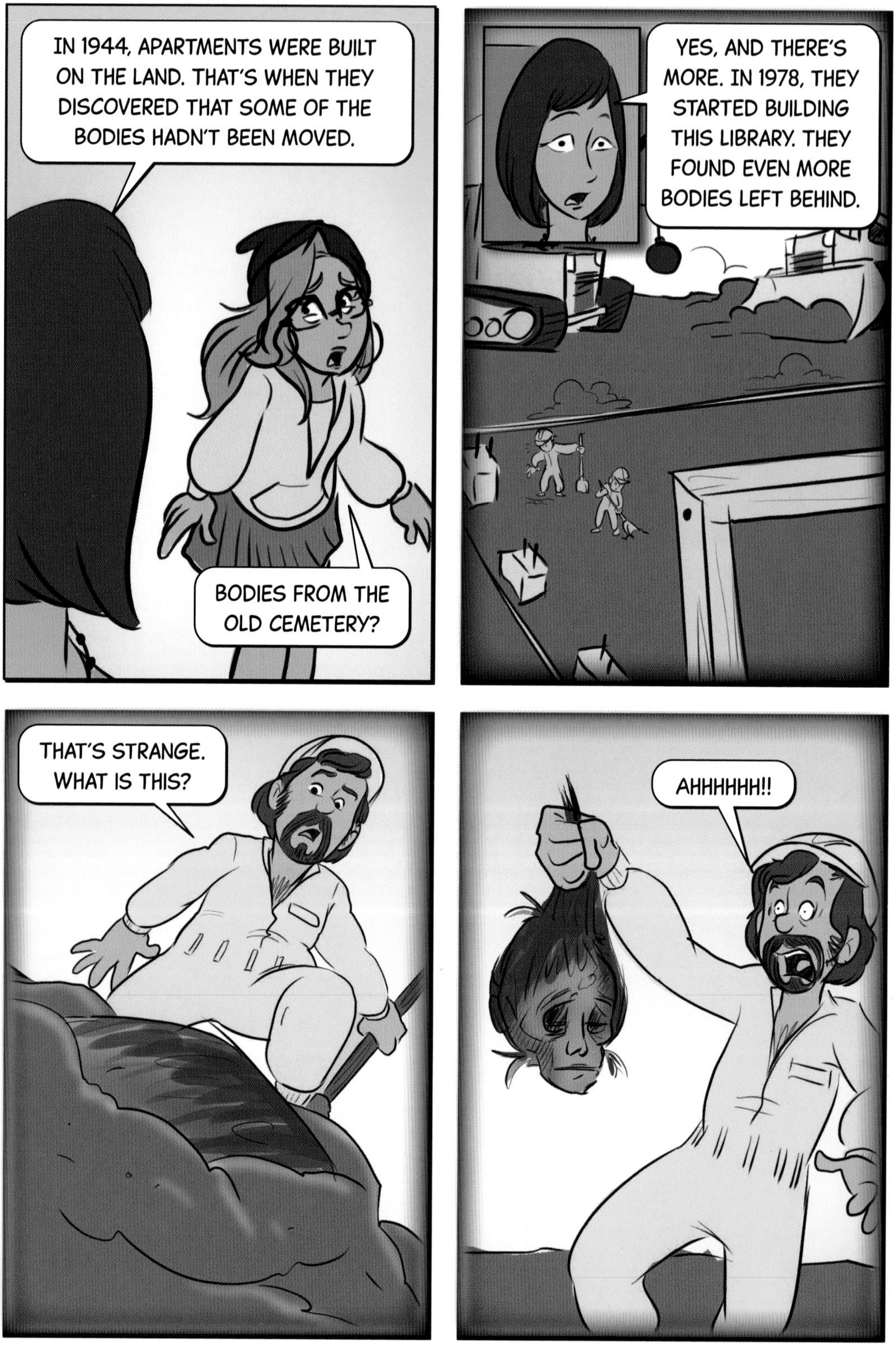
IN 1944, APARTMENTS WERE BUILT ON THE LAND. THAT'S WHEN THEY DISCOVERED THAT SOME OF THE BODIES HADN'T BEEN MOVED.
BODIES FROM THE OLD CEMETERY?
YES, AND THERE'S MORE. IN 1978, THEY STARTED BUILDING THIS LIBRARY. THEY FOUND EVEN MORE BODIES LEFT BEHIND.
THAT'S STRANGE. WHAT IS THIS?
AHHHHHH!!

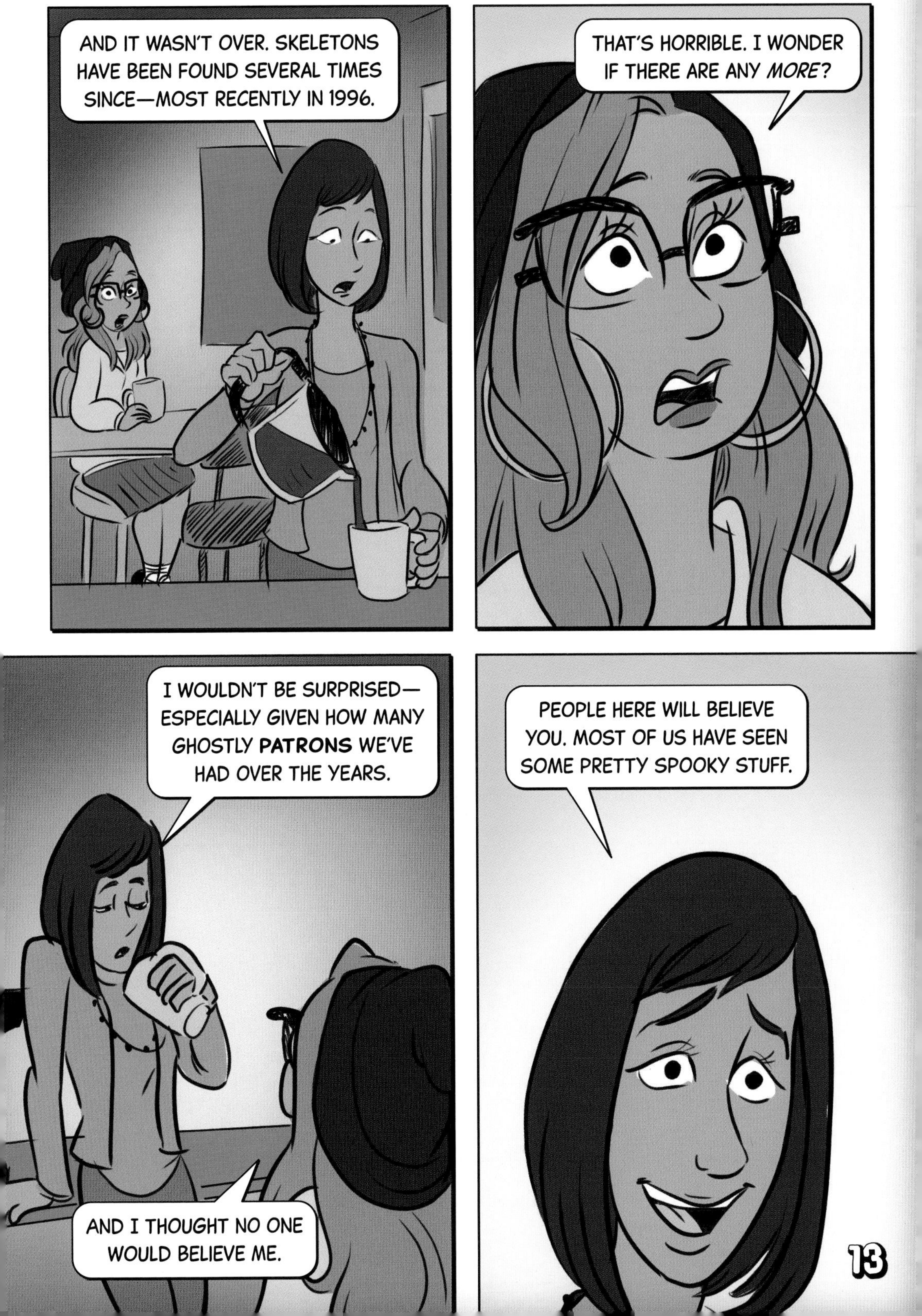
AND IT WASN'T OVER. SKELETONS HAVE BEEN FOUND SEVERAL TIMES SINCE—MOST RECENTLY IN 1996.
THAT'S HORRIBLE. I WONDER IF THERE ARE ANY *MORE*?
I WOULDN'T BE SURPRISED—ESPECIALLY GIVEN HOW MANY GHOSTLY **PATRONS** WE'VE HAD OVER THE YEARS.
AND I THOUGHT NO ONE WOULD BELIEVE ME.
PEOPLE HERE WILL BELIEVE YOU. MOST OF US HAVE SEEN SOME PRETTY SPOOKY STUFF.

GHOST LOG

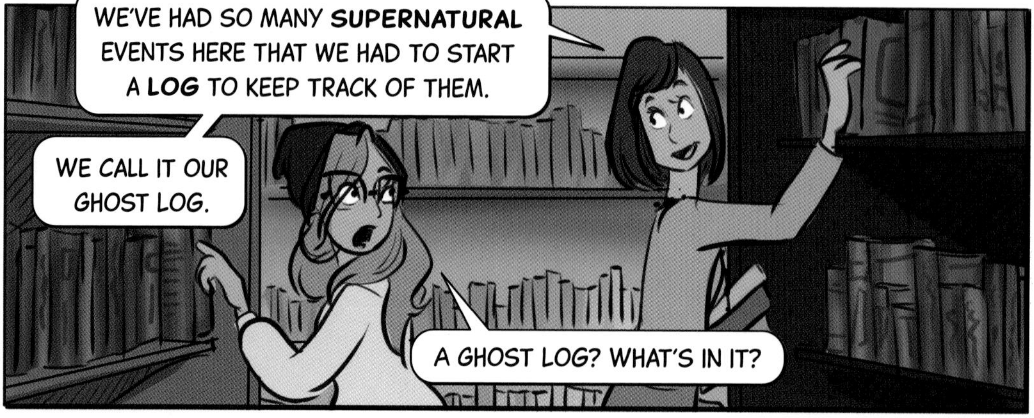
WE'VE HAD SO MANY **SUPERNATURAL** EVENTS HERE THAT WE HAD TO START A **LOG** TO KEEP TRACK OF THEM.
WE CALL IT OUR GHOST LOG.
A GHOST LOG? WHAT'S IN IT?

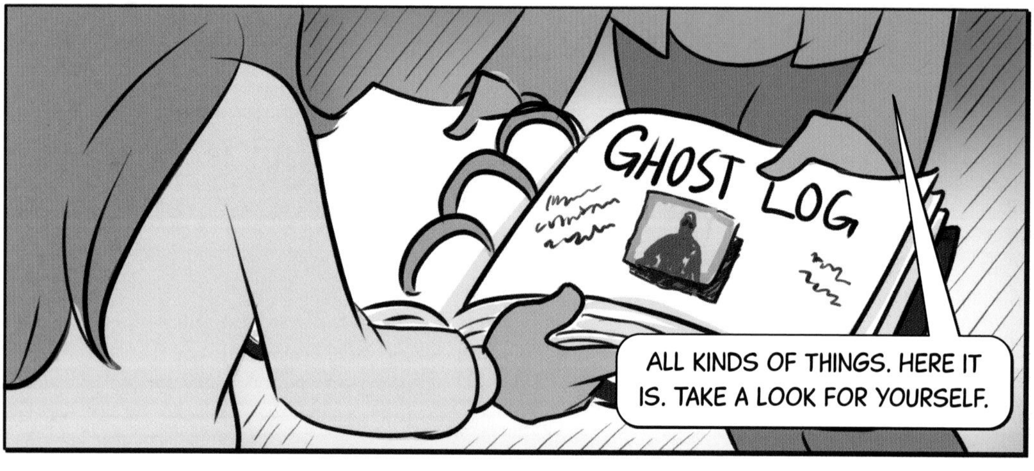
GHOST LOG
ALL KINDS OF THINGS. HERE IT IS. TAKE A LOOK FOR YOURSELF.

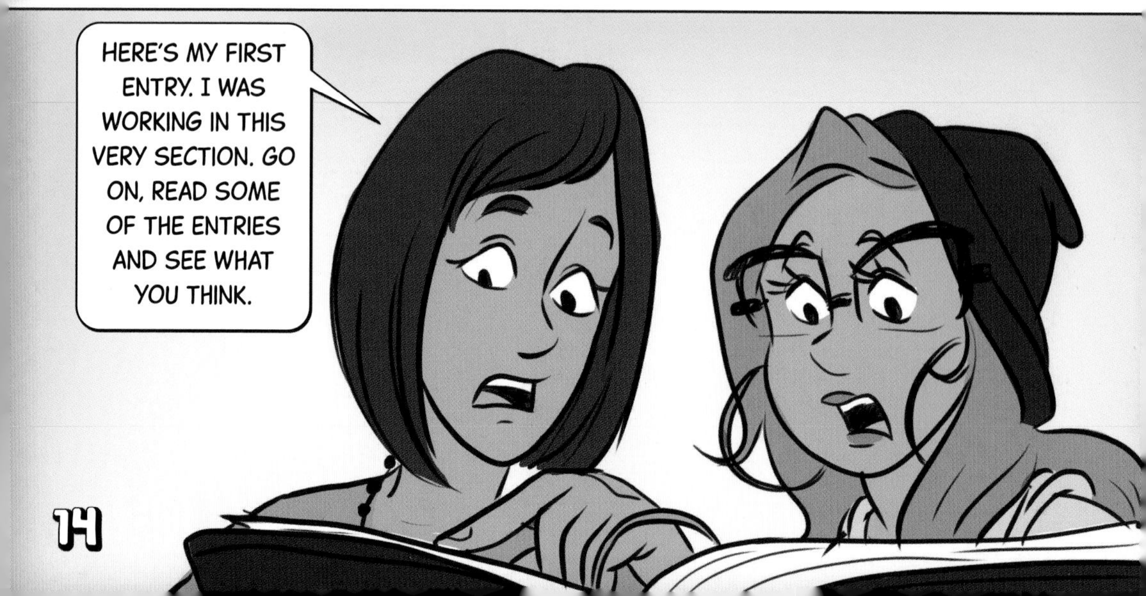
HERE'S MY FIRST ENTRY. I WAS WORKING IN THIS VERY SECTION. GO ON, READ SOME OF THE ENTRIES AND SEE WHAT YOU THINK.

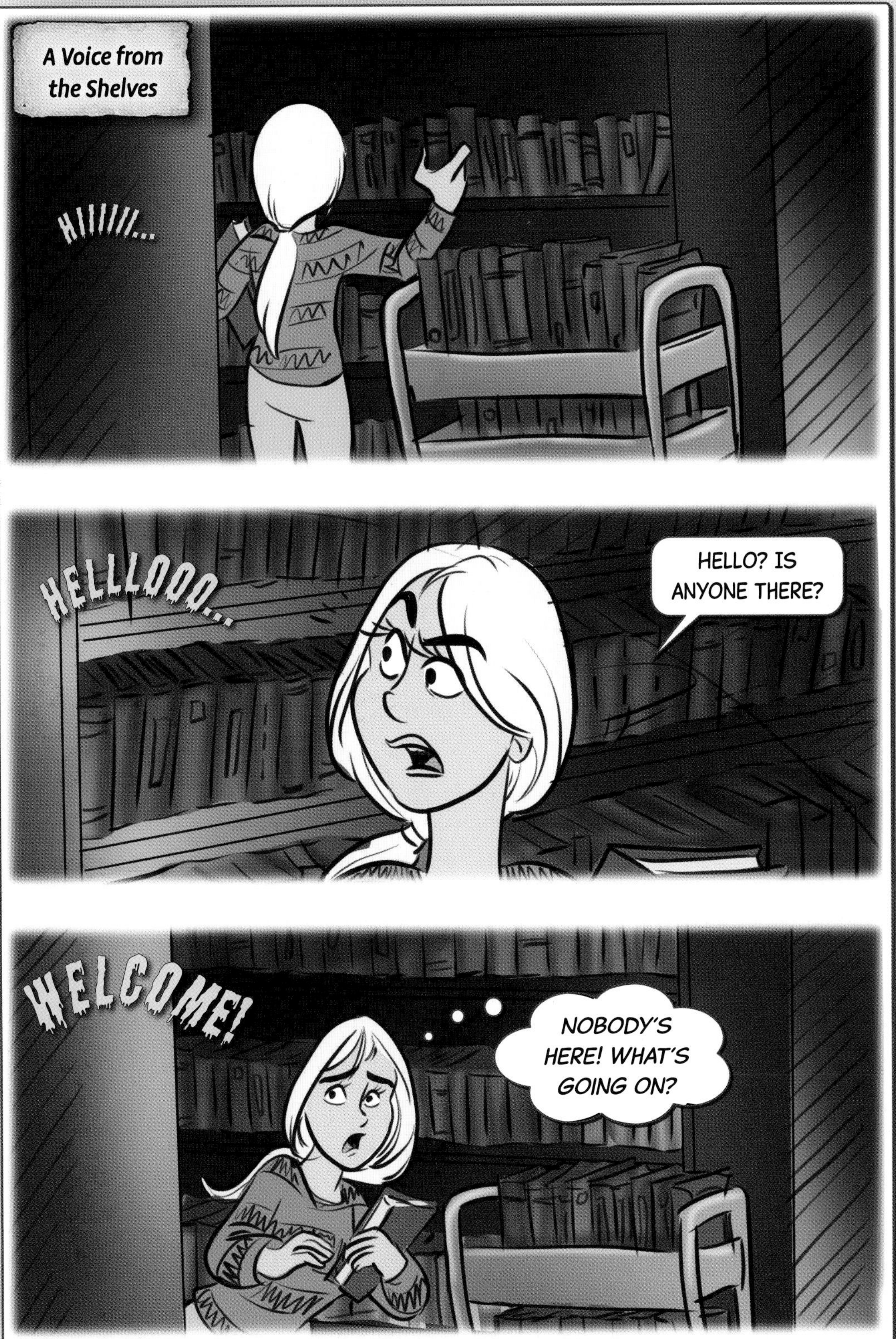
A Voice from the Shelves
HIIIIII...
HELLLOOO...
HELLO? IS ANYONE THERE?
WELCOME!
NOBODY'S HERE! WHAT'S GOING ON?

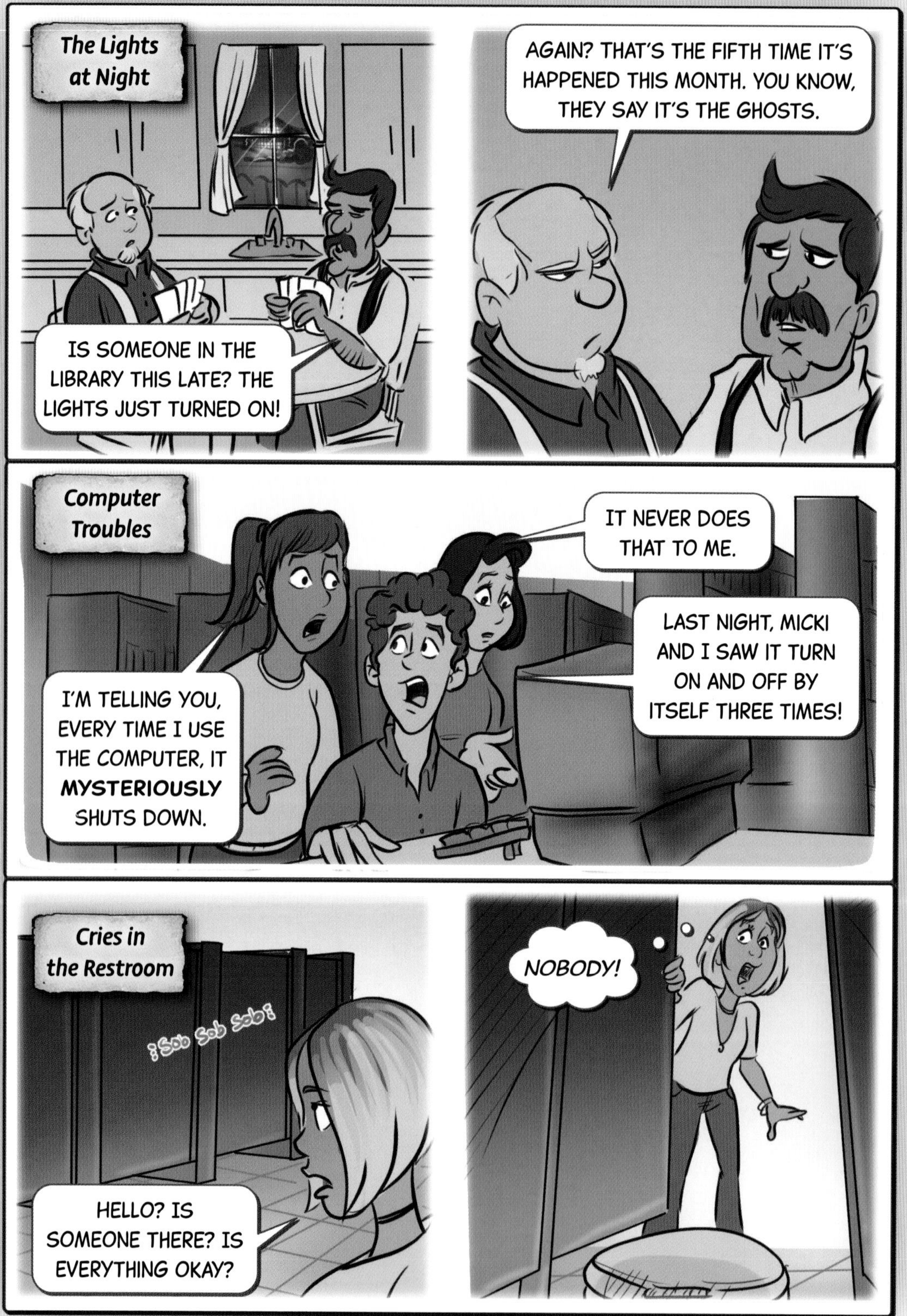
The Lights at Night
IS SOMEONE IN THE LIBRARY THIS LATE? THE LIGHTS JUST TURNED ON!
AGAIN? THAT'S THE FIFTH TIME IT'S HAPPENED THIS MONTH. YOU KNOW, THEY SAY IT'S THE GHOSTS.
Computer Troubles
I'M TELLING YOU, EVERY TIME I USE THE COMPUTER, IT **MYSTERIOUSLY** SHUTS DOWN.
IT NEVER DOES THAT TO ME.
LAST NIGHT, MICKI AND I SAW IT TURN ON AND OFF BY ITSELF THREE TIMES!
Cries in the Restroom
Sob Sob Sob
HELLO? IS SOMEONE THERE? IS EVERYTHING OKAY?
NOBODY!

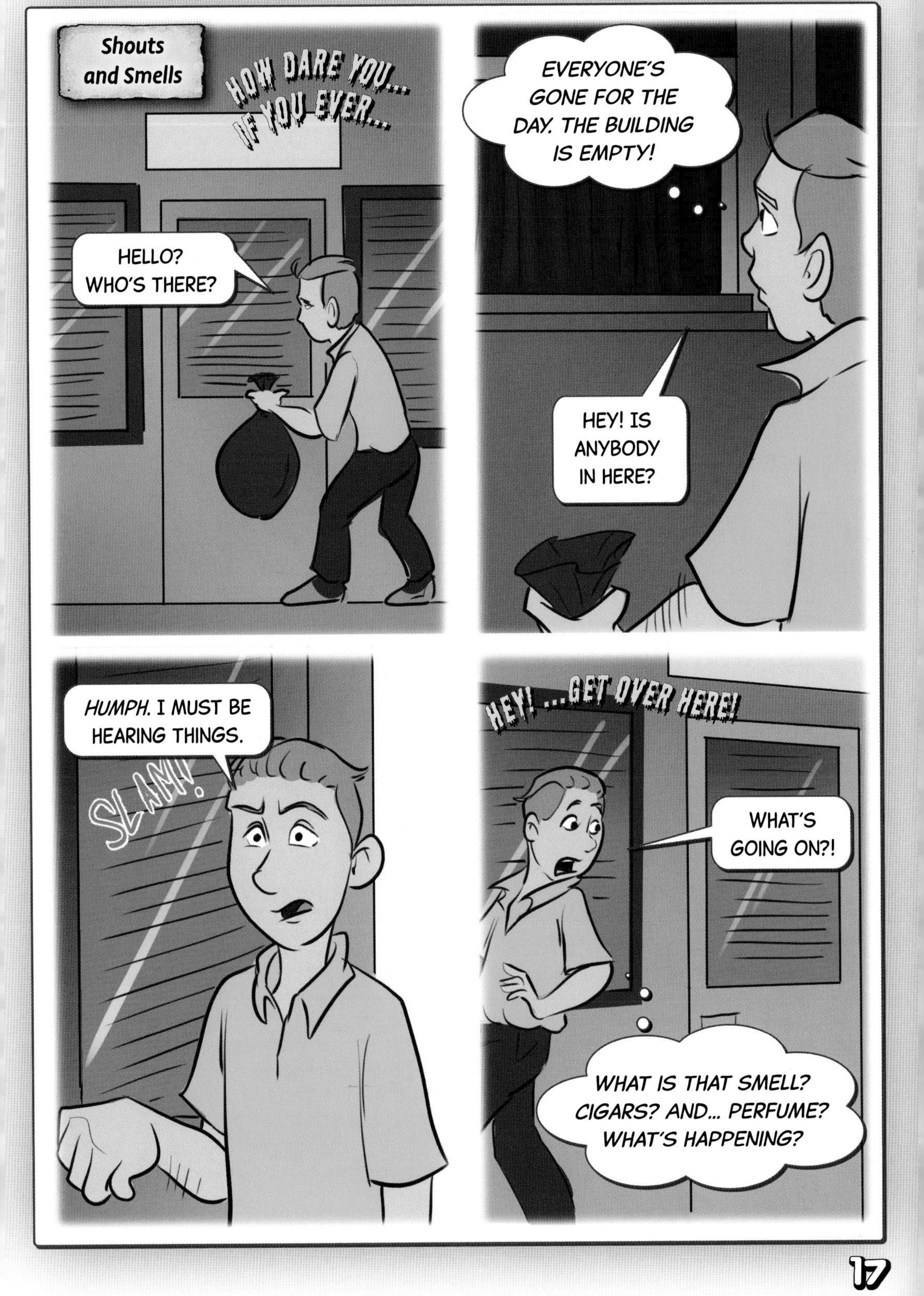
Shouts and Smells
HOW DARE YOU... IF YOU EVER...
HELLO? WHO'S THERE?
EVERYONE'S GONE FOR THE DAY. THE BUILDING IS EMPTY!
HEY! IS ANYBODY IN HERE?
HUMPH. I MUST BE HEARING THINGS.
SLAM!
HEY! ...GET OVER HERE!
WHAT'S GOING ON?!
WHAT IS THAT SMELL? CIGARS? AND... PERFUME? WHAT'S HAPPENING?

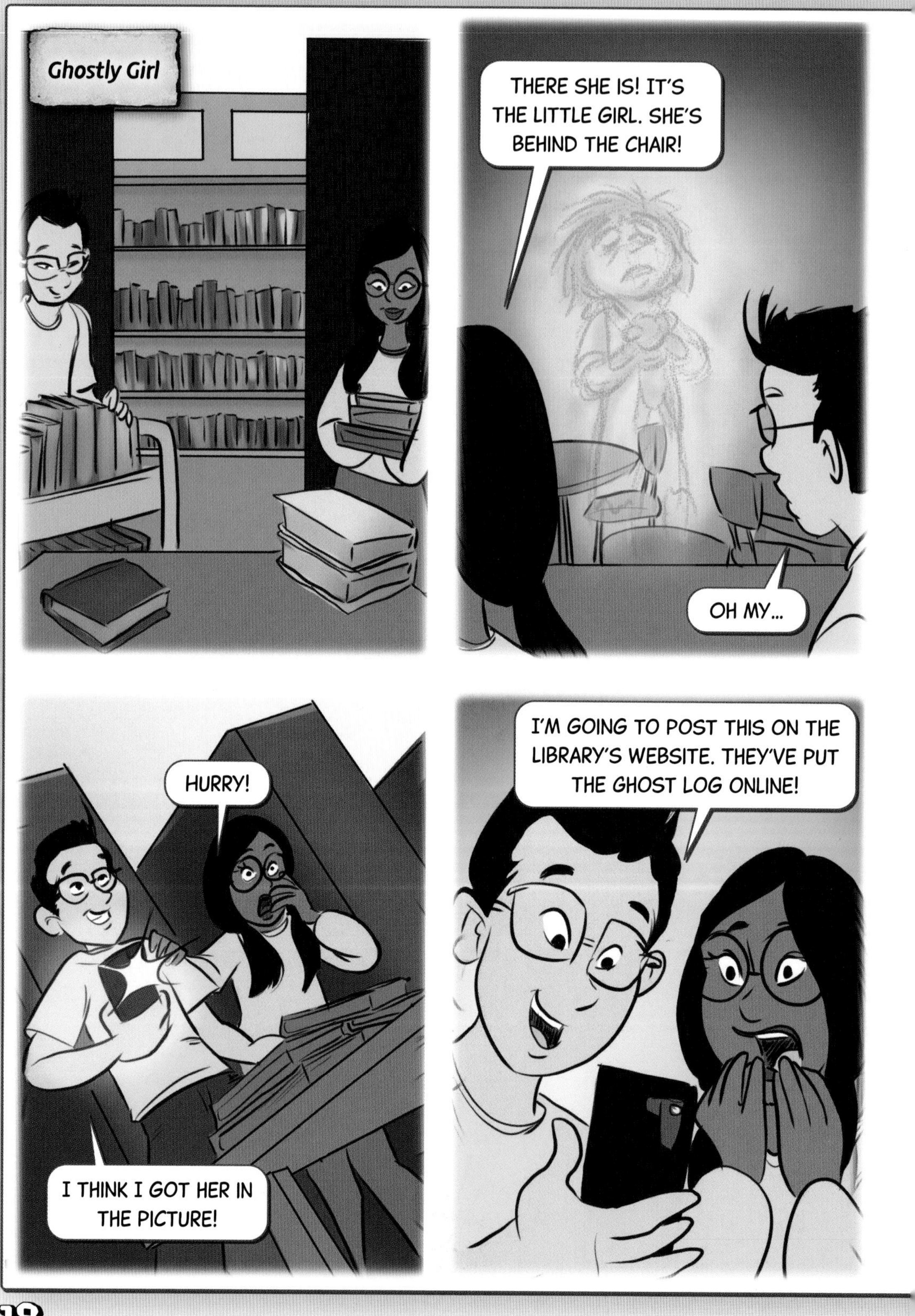
Ghostly Girl
THERE SHE IS! IT'S THE LITTLE GIRL. SHE'S BEHIND THE CHAIR!
OH MY...
HURRY!
I THINK I GOT HER IN THE PICTURE!
I'M GOING TO POST THIS ON THE LIBRARY'S WEBSITE. THEY'VE PUT THE GHOST LOG ONLINE!

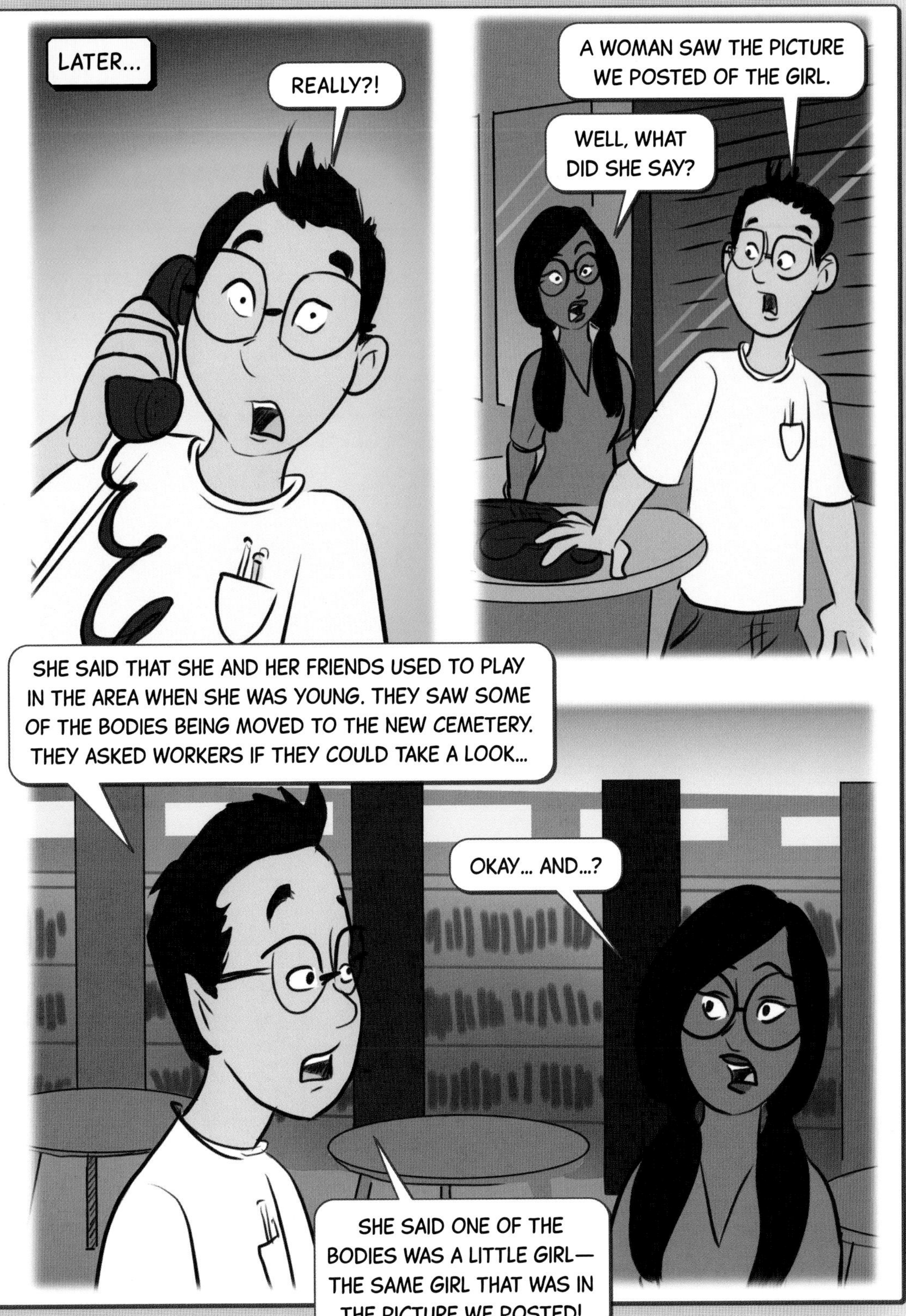
LATER...
REALLY?!
A WOMAN SAW THE PICTURE WE POSTED OF THE GIRL.
WELL, WHAT DID SHE SAY?
SHE SAID THAT SHE AND HER FRIENDS USED TO PLAY IN THE AREA WHEN SHE WAS YOUNG. THEY SAW SOME OF THE BODIES BEING MOVED TO THE NEW CEMETERY. THEY ASKED WORKERS IF THEY COULD TAKE A LOOK...
OKAY... AND...?
SHE SAID ONE OF THE BODIES WAS A LITTLE GIRL— THE SAME GIRL THAT WAS IN THE PICTURE WE POSTED!

STILL RESTLESS SPIRITS

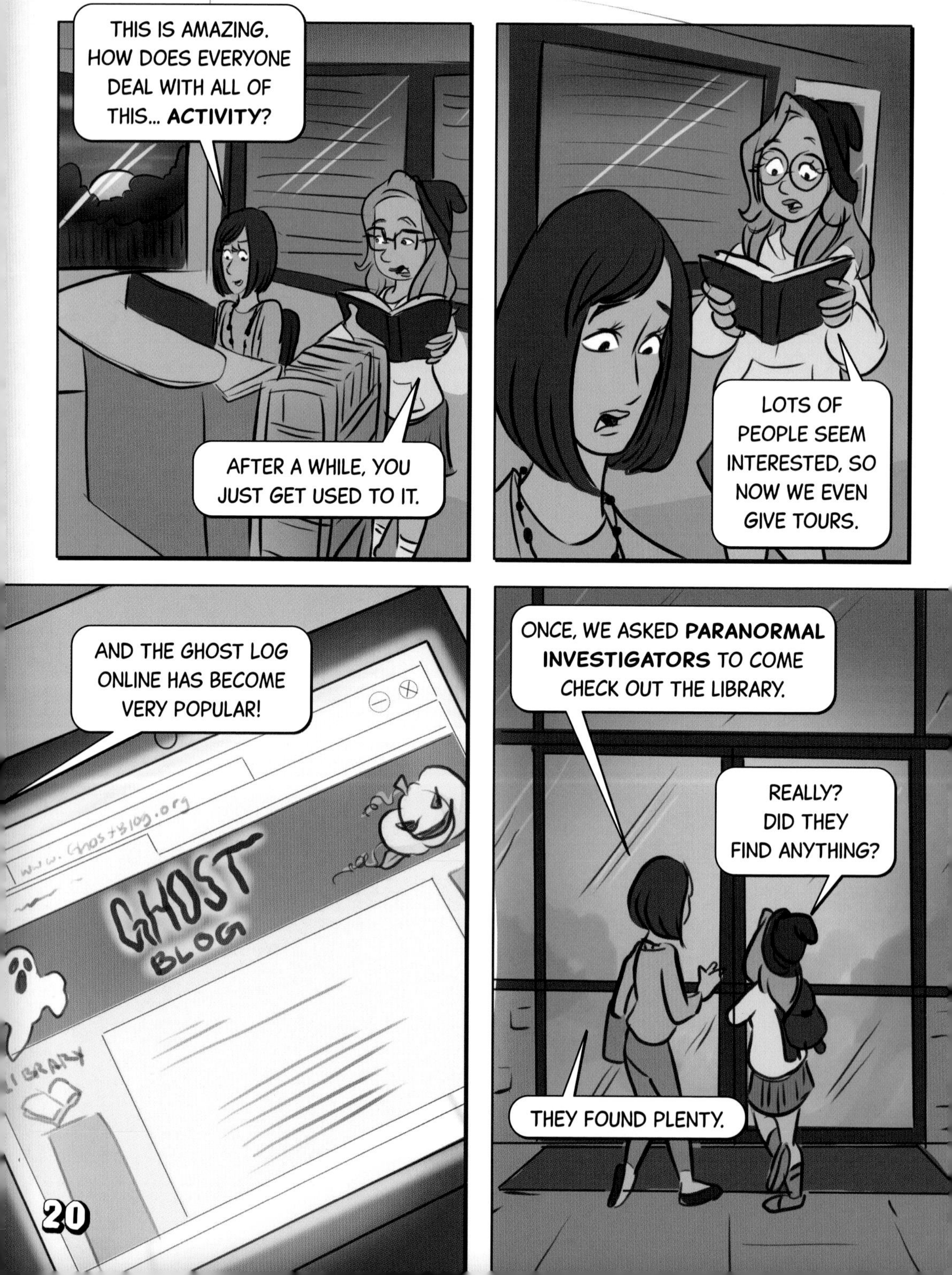

THIS IS AMAZING. HOW DOES EVERYONE DEAL WITH ALL OF THIS... **ACTIVITY**?
AFTER A WHILE, YOU JUST GET USED TO IT.
LOTS OF PEOPLE SEEM INTERESTED, SO NOW WE EVEN GIVE TOURS.
AND THE GHOST LOG ONLINE HAS BECOME VERY POPULAR!
GHOST
BLOG
ONCE, WE ASKED **PARANORMAL INVESTIGATORS** TO COME CHECK OUT THE LIBRARY.
REALLY? DID THEY FIND ANYTHING?
THEY FOUND PLENTY.

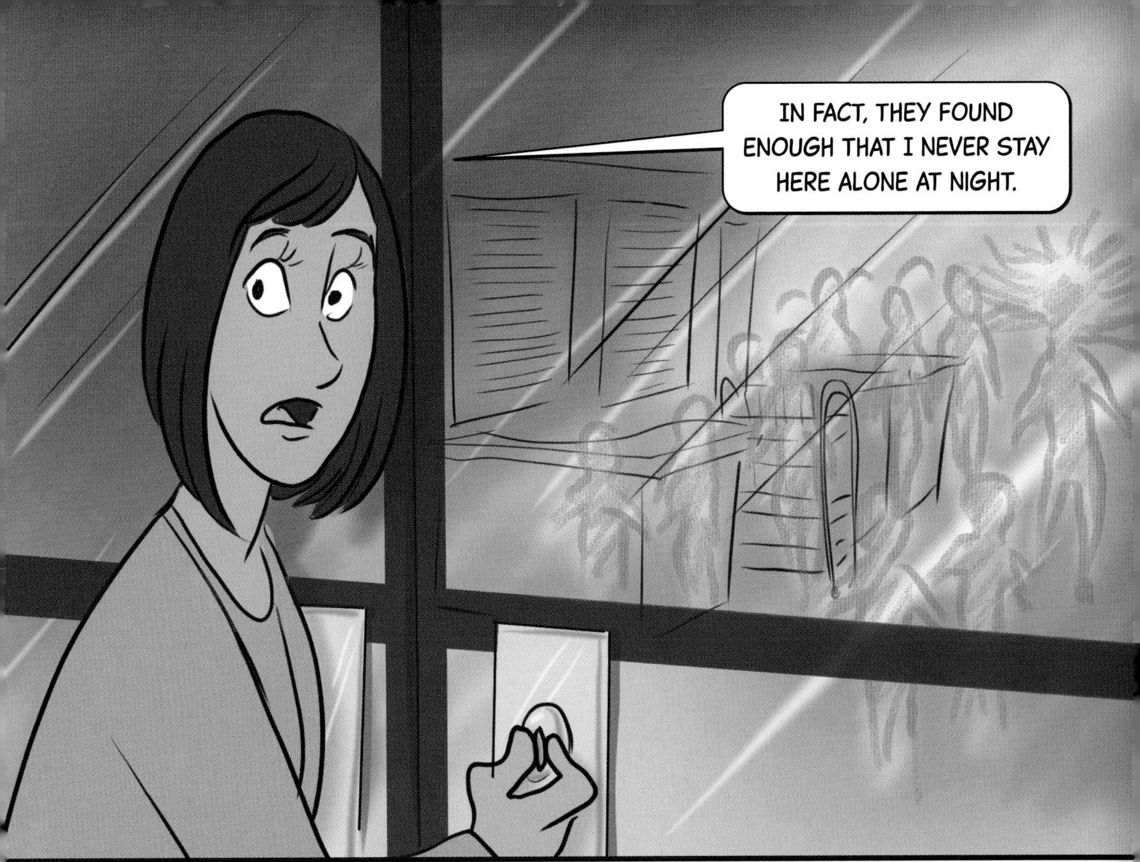
IN FACT, THEY FOUND ENOUGH THAT I NEVER STAY HERE ALONE AT NIGHT.

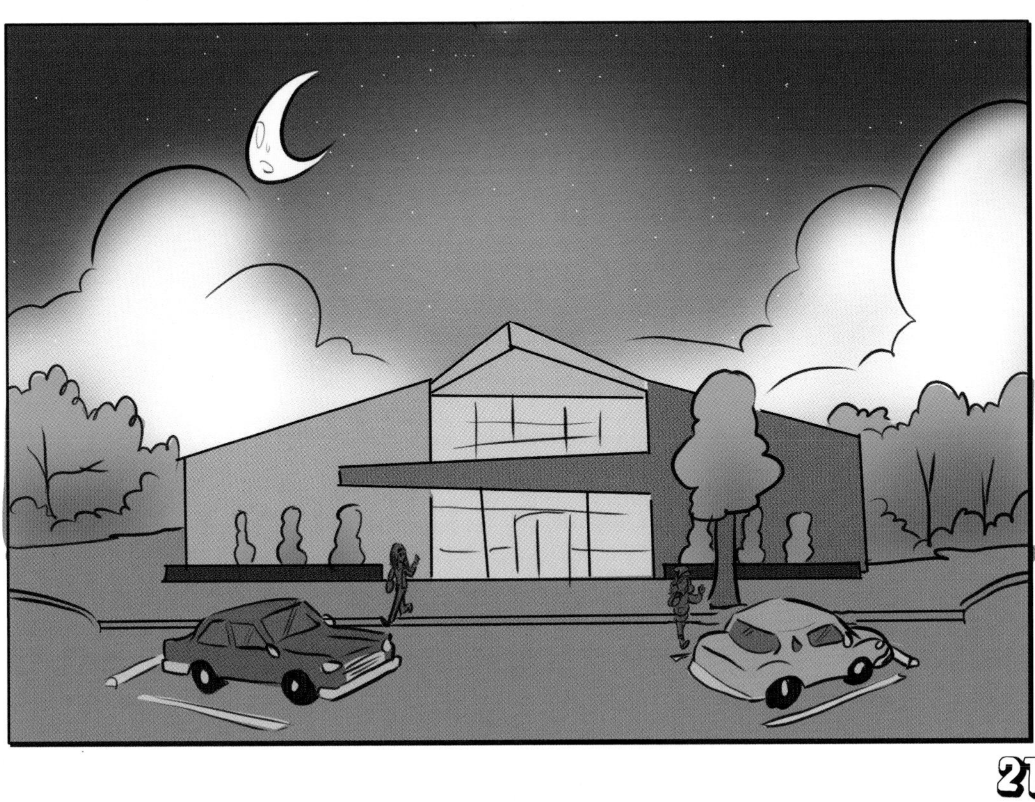

OTHER HAUNTED LIBRARIES

CARNEGIE LIBRARY
PARKERSBURG, WEST VIRGINIA

In 1904, the town of Parkersburg built a library. The library space was turned into the Trans-Allegheny Bookstore in 1985. Today, several ghosts are said to be living in the store. Some people have claimed they tripped over a cat on the store's circular staircase only to turn back and find nothing there. Books fly off the shelves, **overhead** lamps sway back and forth, and lights flicker on and off.

MILLICENT LIBRARY
FAIRHAVEN, MASSACHUSETTS

In 1890, Henry Huttleston Rogers built a library named after his daughter, Millicent, who died when she was just 17 years old. The library has a huge **stained-glass window** that includes a **portrait** of Millicent. The girl remains in the library in another way, too—as a ghost. Patrons claim to have heard Millicent laughing and seen her dancing in the aisles. Paintings of the Rogers family sometimes react to what is being said to them!

GLOSSARY

activity something that has happened

cataloging organizing books by adding them to a list with other important information

cemetery an area of land where dead bodies are buried

log a written record of events

mysteriously in a way that is strange or difficult to understand

outskirts the edges of a town or city that are far from the center

overhead above a person's head

paranormal investigators people who study events or collect information about things that cannot be scientifically explained

patrons people who use the services offered by a business

portrait a painting or other artistic image, usually showing a person's head and shoulders

stained-glass window a window made of colored glass

supernatural having to do with something unusual that breaks the laws of nature

INDEX

READ MORE

Claybourne, Anna. *Don't Read This Book before Bed: Thrills, Chills, and Hauntingly True Stories.* Washington, D.C.: National Geographic (2017).

Oachs, Emily Rose. *Ghosts (Blastoff! Discovery: Investigating the Unexplained).* Minneapolis: Bellwether Media (2019).

Rudolph, Jessica. *Spooky Libraries (Tiptoe into Scary Places).* New York: Bearport (2017).

LEARN MORE ONLINE

1. Go to **www.factsurfer.com**

2. Enter "**Can't Rest in Peace**" into the search box.

3. Click on the cover of this book to see a list of websites.